THE
JULY
BABY

THE
July
BABY

★

Noel Streatfeild

First published in 1959
This edition published in 2023 by Headline Home
an imprint of Headline Publishing Group

1

Cataloguing in Publication Data is available from the British Library

Hardback ISBN 978 1 0354 0851 1
eISBN 978 1 0354 0852 8

Typeset in 14.75/15pt Centaur MT Pro by Jouve (UK), Milton Keynes

Printed and bound in Great Britain by Clays Ltd, Elcograf S.p.A.

MIX
Paper | Supporting
responsible forestry
FSC® C104740

Headline's policy is to use papers that are natural, renewable and recyclable
products and made from wood grown in well-managed forests and other
controlled sources. The logging and manufacturing processes are expected
to conform to the environmental regulations of the country of origin.

HEADLINE PUBLISHING GROUP
An Hachette UK Company
Carmelite House
50 Victoria Embankment
London EC4Y 0DZ

www.headline.co.uk
www.hachette.co.uk

CONTENTS

TELEPHONES have been ringing so the good news has sped round your family and your friends that the July baby has been born. All the usual questions have been asked: How is she? Did she have a bad time? Is it a boy or a girl? How much does it weigh? Who does it look like? But now the moment has arrived when visitors are permitted and everyone is saying to each other 'What are you going to take her?'

As a rule July is a poor month for flowers.

I

The summer ones are too full blown and the autumn ones not yet out. There will of course be roses and perhaps sweet peas and there are always carnations. But the big bunch of flowers from the garden, a popular present had the baby been born a month earlier, are now not likely to be received with rapture by the nurse, for even the best tempered and stoutest-hearted nurse is apt to wilt visibly when flower petals fall on the well-polished or hoovered floor about the patient's bed.

Fortunately in July fruit is at its best, or should be if the weather has been kind: peaches and greengages from the walls, late raspberries and gooseberries, sun-warmed nectarines. But the baby does not eat fruit yet and it is possible for even a vegetarian mother to have too much fruit. So what else is there to bring?

Something to wear is always nice and there are the July sales, but nice as diaphanous

negligées are, friends and relations have more likely been plunging round the July sales buying last-minute cotton frocks or sun suits for their own summer holiday. There are, of course, always presents for the baby, but so few people have the strength of mind to keep those presents until the baby has actually arrived; the temptation to post them beforehand is so overwhelming when both pink and blue are equally correct.

Bath essence, soap and scent for mother

and talcum powder and soap of another kind for baby are lovely presents, and a fortunate mother may find herself stocked up for years to come, but nobody likes to be the sixth person to bring the same present, so what else is there to think of?

Years of visiting mothers and new babies has resulted in this book. What every mother likes to talk about, of course, is baby, and so indeed does father. How would it be, then, if it were possible to buy a book,

not heavy or erudite, but with information about July babies both past and present enclosed within its covers? Here then is such a book.

We start with names. It's an odd thing, but quite a lot of parents have still not decided what to call their baby when they are standing beside the font. One name perhaps has been chosen but it does not go well with the surname, or if two names have been selected they don't sound nice together. So here for parents who are wavering is a list of names all to do with July.

Whether or not you truly believe those columns in the papers that tell you what the stars foretell, most people take a sneaking interest in the signs of the zodiac, so here are the predictions for the babies born under

Cancer and the babies born under Leo. But these alone may not mean much, so this is followed by a list of the distinguished who were born on each day in July, and very surprising reading you may find it. Would you have thought, for instance, that Gina

Lollobrigida, Garibaldi, and Nathaniel Hawthorne were all born under the same sign? Or that Emily Brontë and Henry Moore would share a birthday?

It has been erroneously supposed that mothers in bed at home or in a nursing home or hospital have an immensity of time at their disposal. This is, of course, nonsense. But in minutes between being washed, feeding the baby, being exercised, or just being tidied, it may amuse you to look up the day on which your baby was born, to decide if the child should share the attributes of those others born on the same day; and which of them, if any, you would most like your child to favour.

NAMES
for the
JULY
BABY

THE Romans called July after Julius Caesar. *Julius* means 'downy' and *Caesar* means 'head of hair'. From *Julius* come the boys' names *Julian* and *Jolyon*, and the girls' names *Gillian, Jill, Julia, Juliana, Julie, Juliet* or *Juliette*.

Roman names have held their own a good deal better than Roman numerals. *Roma* or *Romola* mean 'renown'. *Mark, Marcus, Marcellus* and *Martin* all come from Mars, the god of war, and so do the girls' names *Marcella, Marcia, Martine* and *Martina. Anthony* or *Antonia* mean 'inestimable'. *Hadrian* and *Adrian* or *Adrienne* mean 'black'. *Aurelian, Aurea* and *Aurelia* mean 'golden'. *Cato* means 'sagacious'. *Cicero* 'vetch'. *Claudius* means 'lame'; from this name come *Claude, Claudian, Claudia* and *Claudine. Constantine* and *Costin* mean 'firm'. *Cornelius* and *Cornelia* both mean 'regal'. *Fabian* means 'bean-grower', and *Flavia* or *Flavian* would make a suitable name for a red or golden-haired baby because it means 'yellow'. *Horace* or *Horatio* mean 'punctual'. *Justinian* and *Justin, Justina* and *Justine* mean 'just'. The meaning of *Lavinia* has no significance today, for it is 'woman of Lavinia'. *Portia* means 'sow' (fancy that!). *Terence* means 'smooth' and *Titus* 'I honour'. *Virgil* or *Virginia* mean 'spring-like'.

The Anglo-Saxons had a name for July: they called it Meadow-Month. Here are some names to do with meadows. *Leigh* means 'meadow', *Hartley* and *Stanley* mean 'stony meadow'. *Leslie* or *Lesley* mean 'lesser meadow'.

The birthstone for July is a *Ruby,* so it is a very suitable name for a baby girl.

The sign of the zodiac for part of July is Leo the Lion. *Leo, Leon* and *Leonie* mean 'lion.'

Leander means 'lion-man', *Leonard* 'as strong as a lion', *Lionel* 'little lion', and the Welsh names *Llewellyn* and *Llewelyn* mean 'lion-like.'

Each month in the year has an apostle assigned to it. For July the apostle is *Matthew*. *Matthew* means 'gift of Jehovah'. There are quite a lot of saints' days in the July calendar, and perhaps some of them will give you an idea of names for your baby. St Theodoric's Day is the 1st of July. *Theodoric* means 'folk-ruler'; two shortened forms of it which you would not guess are *Derek* and *Terry*.

The 4th of July is St Odo of Canterbury's Day. The name *Odo* means 'rich', and though not used in England now, the German form *Otto* is popular in Germany.

The 9th of July is St Godfrey's Day. *Godfrey* means 'God's peace'. There are quite a lot of names which mean peace. *Absalom* means 'The Divine Father is Peace', *Solomon* 'the peaceable'. *Casimir* 'proclamation of peace'. *Ferry, Frederic* or *Frederick* and *Frederica* 'peaceful ruler'. *Frida, Frieda* and *Irene* 'peace'. *Siegfried* 'victorious peace'. *Geoffrey* and *Jeffrey* 'district-peace'. *Humphrey* 'giant peace'. *Manfred* means

12

'man of peace' and *Renfred* 'judgment of peace'; *Wilfred* or *Wilfrid* 'resolute peace'. *Colin* and *Colman* mean 'dove', as also does *Jemima*. *Columbine* means 'dove-like'.

As you will know, in France, the 14th of July is remembered as Bastille Day, to celebrate the taking of the Bastille Prison in Paris by the mob at the start of the French Revolution in 1789. But did you know that there is a law still on the statute book in France? — though it is no longer rigidly kept, limiting the choice of babies' names to those in the saints' calendar and those appearing in ancient history.

The 15th of July is watched for anxiously by everyone, whether they believe in the superstition or not. If it rains on St Swithin's day it will rain for forty days afterwards, and if the sun shines, there should be forty dazzling days of sunshine. *Swithin* means 'strong', so here are some names with similar meanings. *Valerie* and *Valerian* also mean 'strong', and so does *Drusilla*. *Brian*, *Bryan*, *Brien* and *Dreda* mean 'strength'. *Astrid* means 'God-strength', *Audrey* 'noble strength', *Gertrude* and *Truda* 'spear-strength', *Melisande* and *Millicent* 'work-strong'. *Arnold* 'eagle-strong'. *Gabriel* 'strong man of God' or for girls *Gabriela*, *Gabriella* and *Gabrielle*. *Connor* or *Conor* mean 'great strength'.

The 20th of July is the day of St Margaret. *Margaret* means 'pearl', and there are many forms of it meaning the same thing: *Greta*,

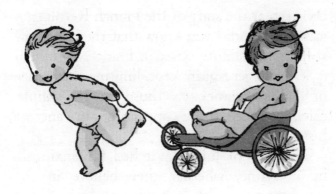

Maisie, Margery, Margot Marguerite, Marjorie, Marjory and *Rita*.

The 22nd of July is St Mary Magdalene's Day. *Mary* means 'wished-for child', and it has many variations – *Maria, Marian, Marianne, Marie, Mariel, Marion, Marlene, Marylyn, Maura, Maureen, Maurine* and *Miriam. Magdalene* means 'woman of Magdala', sometimes it is spelt *Magdalen*, shortened to *Magda* or turned into *Madeleine* or *Madeline*.

The 25th of July is the day of St James. *James* means 'supplanter' and there are other forms of this name – *Hamish, Jacob, Jamie* and *Shamus*, and *Jacobina, Jacqueline, Jacquetta* and *Jamesina* for girls.

St Anne's Day is the 26th of July. *Ann* or

Anne means 'God has favoured me'. *Anita, Anna, Annette* or *Annie* all mean the same thing.

In July the corn is changing from green to gold, and flowers are found in the stubble. What about *Cornflower* or *Poppy* for a July baby girl?

GIFTS
for the
JULY
BABY

17

I F a godparent or well-wisher would like to give a piece of jewellery to the July baby, they should be rich, for the right stone is the ruby. Mothers of July babies may sigh that their offspring has chosen so opulent a birthstone, but rubies, whether you own them or not, have an interesting meaning, for they are the emblem of charity, dignity and divine power, but also they are supposed to repress luxury, which seems very improbable. Here is what Leonardus wrote about rubies in 1750:

'The virtual Power (of the Ruby) is to drive away poisonous and infectious Air, to repress Luxury, to give and preserve the Health of the Body. It takes away vain Thoughts, reconciles Differences among Friends, and makes a mighty Increase of Prosperity.'

The pretty old custom of arranging a vase or bunch of flowers so that it brings a message is almost unknown nowadays. But if your friends revive it and your baby receives a bunch of white lilies, marigolds, and yellow jasmine, here is what it means.

It is predicted (marigolds) that to the baby's purity and sweetness (white lilies) shall be added the qualities of grace and elegance (yellow jasmine).

If your baby was born between the 1st and the 23rd of July read pages 24 and 25, but if between the 24th and the 31st skip ahead to pages 26 and 27.

UNDER
WHAT STARS WAS
MY BABY
BORN?

CANCER
The Crab

22nd June–23rd July

LEO
The Lion

24th July–23rd August

VIRGO
The Virgin

24th August–23rd September

LIBRA
The Scales

24th September–23rd October

SCORPIO
The Scorpion

24th October–22nd November

SAGITTARIUS
The Archer

23rd November–21st December

CAPRICORN
The Sea Goat

22nd December–20th January

AQUARIUS
The Water Bearer

21st January–19th February

PISCES
The Fishes

20th February–20th March

ARIES
The Ram

21st March–20th April

TAURUS
The Bull

21st April–21st May

GEMINI
The Twins

22nd May–21st June

23

Cancer — the Crab
22nd June–23rd July

PEOPLE born under Cancer are magnetic and receptive. Themselves rather self-contained, they draw others to them, and are tenacious in relationships where their strong protective instinct is appealed to strongly enough to turn their will to personal aggrandisement into kindness, sympathy and understanding. Cancer people are reflective, but somewhat uncommunicative. They have orderly habits and low, soft voices. Their

forte is parenthood: they make better fathers
and mothers than people of any other sign.

For the Cancer Baby

Lucky to wear pearls, moonstone, cats-eye,
    aquamarine.
Lucky stone is crystal.
Lucky metal is silver.
The Cancer baby's colour is turquoise.
Lucky numbers are 2 and 7.
Luckiest day is Monday.

Leo — the Lion
24th July–23rd August

TO be born under Leo is to be great-hearted: courageous and compassionate. Leo people are endowed with great stability and power, and their capacity for unswerving action is lessened never by any lack of determination in them but only by impulses of feeling for others. Their power in the world is enormous and of the permanent sort, for they never wield it ruthlessly. They often live in an ideal world of justice and harmony, and do possess the organising ability needed to realise such a world, but wherever there is a choice between what is just and what is generous, feeling will outweigh judgment. Leo, with its emphasis on heart, is considered the best sign of the zodiac under which to be born.

For the Leo Baby

Lucky to wear diamond, jacynth.
Lucky stones are the sparkling ones, like quartz.
Lucky metal is gold.
The Leo baby's colour is orange.
Lucky numbers are 1 and 4.
Luckiest day is Sunday.

BABIES BORN
ON
THE SAME DAY
AS
YOUR BABY

IS there any advantage to be gained from being born on a particular day? Is there any truth in what the astrologers say — that babies born under Cancer are like this, and those born under Leo are like that? Before you decide, here is a list of people, well known both to history and to the present day, for you to look through.

1st   Jean Baptiste, Comte de Rochambeau, 1725. George Sand, 1804. Charles Laughton, 1899. Olivia de Haviland, 1916.

2nd   Christian II of Denmark, 1480. Archbishop Cranmer, 1489. Christopher Gluck, 1714. Henry, 3rd Marquis of Lansdowne, 1780. Franz Kafka, 1883.

3rd   Louis XI of France, 1423.

4th   Queen Philippa of Denmark, 1394. Nathaniel Hawthorne, 1804. Garibaldi, 1807. Stephen Foster, 1826. Gertrude Lawrence, 1900. Gina Lollobrigida, 1927. Prince Michael, 1942.

5th   Joanna de la Tour, Queen of Scotland, 1321. Mrs Sarah Siddons, 1755. The Great Barnum, 1810. Jean Cocteau, 1891.

6th   Nicholas I of Russia, 1796. Emperor Maximilian of Mexico, 1832. Dunoyer de Segonzac, 1884. Andrei Gromyko, 1909.

7th   Gustav Mahler, 1860. Lion Feuch-twanger, 1884. Marc Chagall, 1887. Vittoria De Sica, 1901. Gian Carlo Menotti, 1911.

8th   La Fontaine, 1621. F. V. Zeppelin, 1838. John D. Rockefeller, 1839.

9th   Ann Radcliffe, 1764. Johanna Schopen-hauer, 1766. Henry Hallam, 1777.

10th   James III of Scotland, 1451. John Calvin, 1509. Sir William Blackstone, 1723. Camille Pissarro, 1830. Marcel

Proust, 1871. Lord Gort, 1886. Giorgio de Chirico, 1888.

11th   Robert I of Scotland, 1274. Thomas Bowdler, 1754. Lord Tedder, 1890.

12th   Julius Caesar, 100 B.C. Josiah Wedgwood, 1730. Henry David Thoreau, 1817. Sir William Osler, 1849. Amedeo Modigliani, 1884.

13th   Pope Clement X, 1590. Regnier de Graaf, 1641. Sir George Gilbert Scott, 1811. Eric Portman, 1901.

14th   Emmeline Pankhurst, 1858. Cardinal Mazarin, 1602. Dr Strijdom, 1843.

15th   Inigo Jones, 1573. Rembrandt, 1607. Cardinal Manning, 1808. Lord Northcliffe, 1865.

16th   Saint Clare of Assisi, 1194. Andrea del Sarto, 1486. Sir Joshua Reynolds, 1723. Roald Amundsen, 1872. Trygve Lie, 1896. Ginger Rogers, 1911.

17th   Dr Isaac Watts, 1674. Maxim Litvinov, 1876. Haile Selassie I, 1891. Hardy Amies, 1909. James Cagney, 1899.

18th   Gilbert White, 1720. Thackeray, 1811. W. G. Grace, 1848. Clifford Odets, 1906.

19th   Gilbert Sheldon, Archbishop of
        Canterbury, 1598. Degas, 1834. A. J.
        Cronin, 1896. Dr Louis Boyd Neel,
        1905.

20th   Petrarch, 1304. Sultan Mahmoud II,
        1785. Sir James Phillips Kay-
        Shuttleworth, 1804. Santos-Dumont,
        1873. Dilys Powell, 1901. Sir Edmund
        Hillary, 1919.
21st   Matthew Prior, 1664. Duke of
        Newcastle, 1693. Maria Christina,
        Queen of Spain, 1858. Ernest
        Hemingway, 1898.
22nd   Joan 'Makepeace,' Queen of Scots,
        1210. Simon Langham, Archbishop of

Canterbury, 1376. Anthony Ashley Cooper, 1st Earl of Shaftesbury, 1621. Mendel, 1822. Lord Lyle of Westbourne, 1882. Alan Moorehead, 1910.

23rd   Pope Clement XI, 1649. Coventry Patmore, 1823. Field-Marshal Viscount Alanbrooke, 1883. Stuart Cloete, 1897. Elspeth Josceline Huxley, 1907. Michael Wilding, 1912. Mandy Miller, 1944.

24th   Simón Bolívar, 1783. Alexandre Dumas, 1802. Jean Webster, 1876. Lord Dunsany, 1878. Robert Graves, 1895.

25th   Earl of Balfour, 1848. Elizabeth, Queen of the Belgians, 1876.

26th   Winthrop Mackworth Praed, 1802. Henry Christy, 1810. George Bernard Shaw, 1856. Carl Gustav Jung, 1875. André Chariot, 1882. Aldous Huxley, 1894. Peter Thorneycroft, 1909.

27th   Charlotte Corday, 1768. Thomas Campbell, 1777. Alexandre Dumas the Younger, 1824. Hilaire Belloc, 1870. Sir Geoffrey de Havilland, 1882. Anton Dolin, 1904. Robert Marjolin, 1911.

28th   Sir Hudson Lowe, 1769. Corot, 1796.

Alice Duer Miller, 1874. Selwyn Lloyd, 1904.

29th   Alexis de Tocqueville, 1805. Benito Mussolini, 1883. Duchess of Devonshire, 1895. Dag Hammars-kjöld, 1905. Joseph Grimmond, 1913.

30th   Emily Brontë, 1818. Lord Haldane, 1856. Thorstein Veblen, 1857. Henry Ford, 1863. Henry Moore, 1898.

31st   Princess Augusta of Brunswick, 1737. Thérèse Tallien, 1773. Paul Belloni Du Chaillu, 1835.

THE UPBRINGING OF JULY BABIES OF THE PAST

A CHILD'S CAUL to be sold, in the highest perfection. Enquire at No. 2 Church Street, Minories. To prevent trouble, price £12.

The Times, 1813.

The ANODYNE NECKLACE was one of the most extensively advertised 'quack' remedies of the 18th century. Here is an excerpt from a 'Daily Journal' advertisement:

First put on the Necklace to be worn as other Necklaces are. Then let the Nurse or Mother put upon the end of their Finger a drop or two of the liquid Coral, that is put up along with it, and rub it gently to and fro, now and then over the gums, to make them give way for the easy coming out of the Teeth, and for the pain and anguish to cease. By these means, Numbers of Children, tho' under great severity of Pain, have soon Cut their Teeth with Ease and Safety: and have been Stronger and Healthier at 8 or 9 Months old, than others at 12 or 18 months; by having had (thro' God Almighty's Blessing and Assistance) Fits, Chin-Coughs, Ruptures, Fevers, Convulsions, and other such ailments, incident to Children kept off and prevented to the unspeakable joy of the Parents. This Necklace with the liquid Coral, are sealed up with this seal, with directions. Price both together Five shillings or 48s. a dozen to sell again.

Aveling, *The Chamberlens.*

The ancient Britons had a custom of putting the first morsel of food into their son's

mouth on the point of the father's sword, with the prayer that the child might prove a 'brave warrior', and die on the field of battle.

The Englishwoman's Domestic Magazine, 1860.

What Kind of Food and Diet is proper for young Children, after they are wean'd.

All Kind of Pulse, that grows in Shells or Husks, for Wheat grows in Ears, such as Pease, Beans and Lentils, are to be given very sparingly to a Child, only to accustom him a little to digest the strongest Food;

but they are by no Means proper for him, if he be subject to the Colick, Vertigo, or Epilepsy. But he may often eat the Flesh of wild Fowls, as Larks, Thrushes, Heath-Cocks, Ortolans, Turtle-Doves, Partridges, Ring-Doves, and Pheasants, which took their Name from the River Phasis, whence they came; but not of Geese nor Ducks, which are too hard; nor of Quails, the eating of which, may occasion the Epilepsy, or Falling-Sickness, in those Countries where these Birds live on Hellebore; nor of Woodcocks, which may easily ingender Worms. He may likewise eat the Flesh of tame Fowls, as Chickens, Hens, Pigeons, fat Capons, call'd in Latin, Altiles; Turkey . . .

Among the Flesh of tame Beasts, Veal and Mutton are very proper for a Child; but Pork and Beef, which the Wrestlers eat formerly only at Supper, because they are hard of Digestion, and cause Obstructions, are by no means fit for him to eat, no more than the Flesh of wild Beasts, which are dry, from the Air they breathe, as well as from their Food and Exercise. The Roots that are us'd at Tables, hurt a Child by their Acrimony; and as his hot and moist Temperament ought to be exactly preserv'd, Truffles, which never grow out of the Ground, and have very few fiery and Airy Parts in them, and which are dry, as appears from their Hardness, are very improper and unfit for him.

The Nurse's Guide, by an Eminent Physician, London, 1729.

When a Child is Bewitched.
Stand with the child toward the morning sun, and speak: Be welcome in God's name and sunshine, from whence didst brightly

beam, aid me and my dear child and feign my songs serenely stream. To God the Father sound my praise, help praise the Holy Ghost that he restore my child to health, I praise the heavenly host.

Albertus Magnus, *White and Black Art for Man and Beast*, 13th C., trans. *c.* 1880.

The factory child (vast numbers of these children are hired out at the rate of 1s. 6d. per week), from the very earliest period of its existence, is, in large towns subjected to all the necessary causes for the production of the physical evils, resulting from derangement of the digestive organs. Its food is coarse, and the times of feeding irregular; it is exposed to cold, ill clad, allowed to be filthy. It inhales the impure atmosphere of a badly ventilated and uncleanly house, and the equally impure one of an unpaved and unsoughed street; is allowed to get wet, goes barefoot, no attention is paid to its dietetic comforts, and consequently vast numbers die very young, and the remainder who live exhibit symptoms that they have suffered from neglect and exposure. They have pale and flaccid features, a stunted growth, very often tumid bellies, tender eyes, and other marks that the *primae viae* have been permitted to go wrong. The effect of all the other causes is aided by the abominable practice, so general amongst this class, of cramming their children with quack and patent medicines, to quiet their irritability, increased as it is by their digestive derangement, or the equally pernicious one of giving them gin for the same purpose.

Gaskell, *The Manufacturing Population of England*, 1833

This last summer I was in a gentleman's house where a young child somewhat past four years old could in no wise frame his tongue to say a little short grace, and yet he could roundly rap out so many ugly oaths and those of the newest fashion as some good man of fourscore years old hath never heard named before; and that which was most detestable of all, his father and mother would laugh at it. I much doubt what comfort another day this child shall bring unto them. This child using much the company of serving men and giving good ear to their talk did easily learn, which he shall hardly forget all days of his life hereafter.

Roger Ascham, *The Schoolmaster*, 1570.

PRIVATE TUITION, No. 18, Dorset Gardens, Brighton. – A Married Lady is desirous of taking under her care four or six young Ladies, between the ages of 8 and 14, for the amusement of a well educated Niece, residing with her, who is capable of instructing them grammatically in the English and French languages, Geography, and most of the useful and ornamental branches of education. Terms

50 guineas per ann. No extra charges. Further particulars may be obtained by letter, addressed to S. W., Cross-Keys Tavern, Blackfriars-Road.

The Times, 1809.

DRESSES

One of the prettiest styles, at present in fashion, is what is called a full infant's waist, gathered into a belt, reaching from arm to arm. The back is in one piece, the waist being made by drawing strings, commencing at the belt. The back and waist-piece are joined on the shoulders, and the neck has a narrow binding, through which a bobbin is run, that it may be made loose or tight at pleasure. The belt is usually of insertion, and the sleeves, cut inches in length, have a plain hem, and narrow cambric edging, or are cut from a worked cambric band, a very nice way, as the work is generally more durable. Waist, 6 inches long; 7 inches if the belt is included. A plain skirt, of two breadths, is cut one yard in length, and this allows for a very neat hem, 2 or 3 inches in width.

Opinions vary with regard to the proper length for a baby's dress. The present style, and a graceful one it is, allows even yards in length, or for an embroidered robe, even yards. Others, again, think the weight injurious to a child's feet and limbs, and do not allow more than three quarters of a yard, all told. We think our first measurement a good medium, though, of course, it is a matter for private taste, judgment, and means to decide.

The Nursery Basket, New York, 1854.

For an Infant of a Year old in a Fever, or, as it commonly happens, tormented with the Gripes, we may prescribe as follows: Simple Powder of Crab's Claws one Dram, Crab's Eyes prepared two Scruples, Cochineal six Grains, reduce them to a very fine Powder, and divide them into six Papers. The Infant may take one of these Doses immediately, and repeat it, if necessary, two Hours afterwards, and then once in four Hours, except when asleep, for the two first Days.

Martyn, *A Treatise of the Acute Diseases of Infants*, 1742.

DISTINGUISHED
JULY
BABIES

GEORGE SAND
born July 1804.

I WAS two years old when a maid let me fall from her arms against the angle of a fireplace. My forehead was hurt, and I was afraid. This commotion, this shock to the nervous system opened my spirit to a sensation of life, and I still see the reddish marble of the fireplace, my blood flowing, and the startled face of my maid. I distinctly recall too the visit of the doctor, the leeches they put behind my ear, the anxiety of my mother, and that the maid was dismissed for being drunk. We left that house, and I do not know where it was situated. I never went back to it, but if it still exists, it seems to me that I should recognize it.

It is not then astonishing that I recall perfectly the apartment we occupied in rue Grange-Bateliere a year later. My precise and uninterrupted memories date from there. But from the fireplace accident to the age of three years, I retrace only an indeterminate sequence of hours spent in my little bed without sleeping, and filled by the contemplation of some fold in the curtain or some flower on the wallpaper of the room. I remember too that the flight of the flies and their buzzing interested me a great deal, and that I often saw objects double. I find it impossible to explain this, but several people have told me that they experienced the same phenomenon in their early childhood. It was especially candle flames that I saw double, and I was aware of the illusion without being able to escape from it. I think really that this illusion was one of the pale amusements of my captivity in the cradle and that cradle life seemed to me extraordinarily long and plunged in soft boredom.

My mother began teaching me when I was very young, and my mind made no resistance, but it did nothing on its own initiative. It might have been very backward if it had been left alone. I walked at ten months of age, and I spoke quite late, but once I had begun to say a few words I learned all the words very fast and at four years of age I could read very well. So could my cousin Clotilde, who was taught, like me, by our two mothers alternating. They taught us too some prayers, and I recall that I recited them without hesitating from beginning to end without understanding anything of them except the words they had us say when our heads were laid on the same pillow: 'My God, I give you my heart.' I do not know why I understood that better than the rest, for there is a great deal of philosophy in those few words, but I did in fact understand it, and it was the only place

in my prayer where I had an idea of God
and of myself.

This was translated from the
autobiography of George Sand.

MRS SIDDONS
born July 1755.

I am unable to state the exact date of Mrs
Siddons' first appearance on the stage, but it
must have been very early; for the company
was offended at her appearance of childhood,
and was for some time shaken with uproar.
The timid debutante was about to retire,

when her mother, with characteristic decision, led her to the front of the stage, and made her repeat the fable of the 'Boys and the Frogs,' which not only appeased the audience, but produced thunders of applause.

Campbell, *Life of Mrs Siddons,* 1834.

EMILY BRONTË
born July 1818.

Here is an extract from the school register of the Clergy Daughters' School at Casterton:

'Emily Brontë. Entered November 25, 1824, aged 5¾. Reads very prettily, and works a little. Left June 1, 1825. Subsequent career . . . Governess.'

Journal of Education, 1900.

NATHANIEL HAWTHORNE
born July 1804.

Here is an extract from his first diary:

'This morning the bucket got off the chain and dropped back into the well. I wanted to go down on the stones and get it. Mother would not consent, for fear the wall might cave in, but hired Samuel Shane to go down. In the goodness of her heart, she thought the

son of old Mrs Shane not quite so valuable as the son of the widow Hawthorne. God bless her for all her love for me, though it may be some selfish. We are to have a pump in the well after this mishap.'

Pickard, *Hawthorne's First Diary*, 1897.

German philosopher and mathematician
born July 1646.

I remember but two circumstances con-
nected with my father. The first was, that,
as I early learned to read, he took great pains
to awaken in me an interest in history, both
sacred and profane. This he endeavoured to
do, partly by means of a small book in the
German language, and partly by repeated oral
recitations; and with such a favourable result,
as led him to indulge the brightest anticipations
of my future progress. The other circumstance
was in fact remarkable, and still remains as
fresh in my memory as if it had happened but
yesterday. The day was Sunday; and my
mother had gone to hear the morning sermon.
But my father lay sick in his bed. Before being
fully dressed, I was playing about the stove,
and tripping it up and down a bench that
stood between the wall and the table. The
nursery-maid wishing to put on my clothes, I,
full of my pranks, mounted the table; and,
upon her attempting to seize me, I stepped
backwards, and fell down upon the pavement.

My father and the maid scream out: they look, and see me laughing at them, unhurt, though at no less a distance than three paces from the table. In this, my father recognized the special favor of God, and straightway dispatched some one with a note to the church, that, according to custom, thanks might be offered after the service. This affair became the subject

of remark throughout the town; and my father, from this accident, or I know not what other dreams and prognostics, was led to indulge so great expectations of me, as often to expose himself to the playful satire of his friends.

Leibnitz, *Personal Recollections.*

HENRY GRATTAN
born July 1746.

When very young, Mr Grattan had been frightened by stories of ghosts and hobgoblins, which nurses are in the habit of relating to children, so much so, as to affect his nerves to the highest degree. He could not bear being left alone, or remaining long without any person, in the dark. This feeling he determined to overcome, and he adopted a bold plan. In the dead of night he used to resort to a churchyard near his father's house, and there he used to sit upon the gravestones, whilst the perspiration poured down his face, but by these efforts he at length succeeded and overcame his nervous sensation. This certainly was a strong proof of courage in a child.

Memoirs of Henry Grattan, by his Son, 1848.

MADAME SCHOPENHAUER
born July 1766.

'Now, you rogues, can you eat well?' was the first speech that our new doctor addressed to my sister and myself when we were placed before him. 'Well, you must soon leave that off, and hunger, hunger till your soul whistles,' said he, in reply to my answer in the affirmative: he then went on to prescribe weak broth, tea without any milk, white bread, biscuits, and currant jelly, as the requisite diet

which we were to be put upon preparatory to the grand experiment. Half the city awaited the issue with intense curiosity, and many good people felt themselves much scandalised at the whole affair.

With what wearisome circumstantiality

was every thing performed in those days that we now dispatch as well and as safely with the greatest ease, almost, indeed, without noticing it! how cumbersome was life then with all its duties! The most anxious mother would now-a-days tell only her most intimate friend, and that in a casual manner, that her children had been vaccinated in the course of the morning; but with us the whole house was put into a state of alarm on that important day.

Our parents, we three unfortunate dramatis personae, Dr Wolf, Herr Nixius our family surgeon, Kasche, and the servant maid Florentine, were all packed, one miserable April day, into a coach and driven to the most distant corner of the city, into the midst of a dirty back-yard belonging to a shabby house, the threshold of which we durst not cross, because we had been informed that on the fourth storey there were some children whom Dr Wolf pronounced to be in a dangerous state.

There in the open air we three poor little girls sat shivering with cold and fright, with geese, hens, and curious pigs, cackling and grunting round us. Dr Wolf made eight little punctures on each of us with a gold needle dipped into the pus of the small-pox, two on each hand, between the index finger and the thumb, and two on each knee; it was by no means the smallest part of my sufferings that we had to sit a long while before every body, with our knees bare to allow the puss to dry in; this part of the operation seemed to me very indecent as well as disagreeable on account of the inclemency of the weather.

The whole performance was conducted with a tedious regard to minute details that would hardly be credited in the present day. Fresh virus had to be fetched from the patients up-stairs for each of our eight wounds, consequently Mr Nixius was obliged to go four and twenty times to the fourth storey of the crazy old building: Florentine stood at the door to receive the needle from him, which she handed to Kasche, who was placed a few steps from her; she passed it on to my mother, who at last gave it into Dr Wolf's hand.

We returned home from our miserable

expedition half dead, or at least we thought ourselves so; we would gladly have gone at once to bed, but this was not allowed, for the physician's orders were that we should play and make ourselves merry. Every day was spent in recreation and walking, till at last we became too weak in consequence of the abstemious diet on which we had been put. Dr Wolf felt himself at length under the necessity of allowing us some good broth in order to bring the pustules to a head, and from that time my sisters improved rapidly; the dreaded malady passed lightly over them without leaving the least trace of its presence behind.

With me it fared far otherwise; I felt myself in great pain, and covered all over with pustules, and the incessant but anxious care which Dr Wolf took of me showed but too plainly how dangerous he considered my case to be.

My recovery under these circumstances must be attributed to the great attention I received from this humane and benevolent man; for several days he scarcely left the house, and no young princess could have experienced from the court physician more unremitting care than I received from Dr Wolf.

Youthful Life by Madame Schopenhauer.
Translated 1847.

ROBERT CHAMBERS
born July 1802.

My first two years of schooling were spent amidst the crowd of children attending Mr Gray's seminary. On the easy terms of two shillings and twopence per quarter I was well grounded by the master and his helper in English. The entire expense must have been only about eighteen shillings — a fact sufficient to explain how Scotch people of the middle class appear to be so well educated in comparison with their southern compatriots. It was prior to the time when the intellectual system was introduced. We were taught to read the Bible and Barrie's *Collection,* and to spell words. No attempt was made to enlighten us as to the meaning of any of the lessons. The most distressing part of our school exercises consisted in learning by heart the Catechism of the Westminster Assembly of Divines, a document which it was impossible for any person under maturity to understand, or to view in any other light than as a torture. It was a strange, rough, noisy, crowded scene this burgh school. No refinement of any kind appeared in it. Nothing kept the boys in any sort of order but flagellation with the tawse. Many people thought the master did not punish enough. This idea, in fact, was the cause of an act of wild justice, which I saw executed one day in the school.

The reader must imagine the school-hum going on in a dull monotone, when suddenly the door burst open, and in walked a middle-aged woman of the humbler class, carrying something in her right hand under her apron. The school sunk into silence in an instant. With flashing eyes and excited visage, she called out: 'Where is Jock Forsyth?' Jock had maltreated a son of hers on the green, and she had come to inflict vengeance upon him before the whole school. Jock's conscious soul trembled at the sight, and she had no difficulty in detecting him. Ere the master had recovered from the astonishment which her intrusion had created, the fell virago had pounced upon the culprit, had dragged him into the middle of the floor, and there began to belabour him with the domestic tawse, which she had brought for the purpose.

The screams of the boy, the anxious entreaties of the master, with his constant 'Wifie, wifie, be quiet, be quiet,' and the agitated feeling which began to pervade the school, formed a scene which defies words to paint it. Nor did Meg desist till she had given

Master Forsyth reason to remember her to the latest day of his existence. She then took her departure, only remarking to Mr Gray, as she prepared to close the door: 'Jock Forsyth will no' meddle with my Jamie again in a hurry.'

Memoir of Robert Chambers, 1872.

GAMES
for the
JULY
BABY

THE following explains its own theatrical character:

I got a little manikin, I set him on my thoomikin;

I saddled him, I bridled him, and sent him to the tooniken;

I coffed a pair o' garters, to tie his little hosiken;

I coffed a pocket-napkin to dight his little nosiken;

I sent him to the garden, to fetch a pund o' sage,

And fand him in the kitchen-neuk, kissin' little Madge!

Popular Rhymes of Scotland, W. & R. Chambers, 1842.

SEE-SAW

A common game, children vacillating on either
end of a plank supported on its centre. While
enjoying this recreation, they have a song of
appropriate cadence, the burden of which is:

> Titty cum tawtay,
> The ducks in the water:
> Titty cum tawtay,
> The geese follow after.

Popular Rhymes and Nursery Tales,
collected by Halliwell, 1849.

QUEEN ANNE

Queen Anne, Queen Anne, who sits on
her throne,
As fair as a lily, as white as a swan;

The king sends you three letters,
And begs you'll read one.

This is said by all the children but one, who
represents the Queen, they having previously
hid a ball upon one of their number. The
Queen answers,

I cannot read one unless I read all,
So pray, . . . , deliver the ball.

Naming any child she pleases. If she guesses
rightly the child who has the ball takes her
place as Queen. If wrongly, the child who has
the ball says,

The ball is mine, and none of thine,
So you, proud Queen, may sit on your
    throne,
While we, your messengers, go and come.

Popular Rhymes and Nursery Tales,
Halliwell, 1849.

A JULY
CHILD
IN
FICTION

I WAS a dainty child ('more nice than wise,' as my nursemaid contemptuously expressed it), and I shrank from our coarse, country-bred servants. Their boisterous movements, loud voices, and rough hands, were disagreeable to me. The mingling of shyness and pride with which I regarded the inmates of our kitchen, would, had I had no refuge from their company, have grown into positive hatred. But this tendency to a morbid tone of mind was greatly counteracted by my visits to Mortlands. At home, the servants alternately scolded and spoiled me. They were, I believe, amused with my little disdainful airs, as they might have been amused at the shrinking of some delicate little animal from their rough, but not unkindly, touch. I had not the resource of solitude at will (which would have been far less injurious to a character like mine), for it would not have been safe to let a child of my years wander alone about the farm.

Frances Trollope, *Anne Furness*, 1871.

It is reported of him, that before the first year of his infancy was elapsed, he used very often, immediately after being dressed, in the midst of the caresses which were bestowed upon him by his mother while she indulged herself in the contemplation of her own happiness, all of a sudden to alarm her with a fit of shrieks and cries, which continued with great violence till he was stripped to the skin with the utmost expedition by order of his affrighted parent, who thought his tender body was tortured by the misapplication of some unlucky pin; and when he had given them all this disturbance and unnecessary trouble, he would lie sprawling and laughing in their faces as if he ridiculed the impertinence of their concern. Nay it is affirmed, that one day, when an old woman who attended in the nursery had by stealth conveyed a bottle of cordial waters to her mouth, he pulled his nurse by the sleeve, and by a slight glance detecting the theft, tipt her the wink with a particular slyness of countenance, as if he had said with a sneer, 'Ay, ay, that is what you must all come to.' But these instances of reflection in a babe nine months old are so incredible, that I look upon them as *ex post facto* observations, founded upon imaginary recollection, when he was in a more advanced age, and his peculiarities of temper became much more remarkable . . .

Smollett, *The Adventures of Peregrine Pickle*, 1751.

LETTERS
from
JULY
CHILDREN

Nohant, 24th February, 1815.

OH ! yes, dear mother, I kiss you, I wait for you, I want you and I am dying of impatience to see you here. Good heavens, how worried you are about me! Don't be anxious, dear little mother. I go out walking, I run, I come and go, I have fun, I eat well, sleep better and think of you still more.

Good-bye, dear mother; don't, then, do any worrying at all. I love you with all my heart

Aurore.
Translation of a letter by George Sand, born July 1804.

24th March, 1819.

Dear Uncle,

I suppose you have not heard of the death of Mr Tarbox and his wife, who were frozen to death on Wednesday last. They were brought from the Cape on Saturday, and buried from Captain Dingley's on Sunday. The snow is going off very fast, and I don't think we shall have much more sleighing. I hope we shall not, for I am tired of winter.

You ordered me to write as well as I could, but this is bad paper. I am writing with a bad pen, and am in a hurry, as I am going to Portland at noon with Mr Leach.

Your affectionate nephew,
Nathaniel Hawthorne.

P.S. This paper is two cents a sheet.

(Hawthorne was born July, 1804.)

12th February, 1818.

My dear mama,

I hope you are quite well. I have given my dear Grandmama a kiss. My Aunt Ritchie is very good to me. I like Chiswick, there are so many good Boys to play with. St James's Park is a very fine place. St Paul's Church too I like very much. It is a finer place than I expected. I hope Captain Smyth is well; give my love to him and tell him he must bring you home to your affectionate little son,

William Thackeray.
From The Letters of Anne Thackeray Ritchie, published by John Murray.

RHYMES
for the
JULY
BABY

HOT July brings thunder-showers,
Apricots and gilly-flowers.
                Sara Coleridge (1802–1852).

Twinkle, twinkle, little star,
How I wonder what you are!
Up above the world so high,
Like a diamond in the sky.

When the blazing sun is gone,
When he nothing shines upon,
Then you show your little light,
Twinkle, twinkle, all the night.

Then the traveller in the dark
Thanks you for your tiny spark:

He could not see which way to go,
If you did not twinkle so.

In the dark blue sky you keep,
And often through my curtains peep,
For you never shut your eye,
Till the sun is in the sky.

As your bright and tiny spark
Lights the traveller in the dark,
Though I know not what you are,
Twinkle, twinkle, little star.

Easy Rhymes and Simple Poems,
London: 1864.

Hush-a-by baby,
　　On the tree top,
When the wind blows
　　The cradle will rock;
When the bough breaks,
　　The cradle will fall,

Down tumbles baby,
Cradle and all.
Mother Goose's Melody,
London: 1817.

A PRAYER

Lord, look upon a little child,
By nature sinful, rude, and wild;
Oh! Lay Thy gracious hands on me,
And make me all I ought to be.
Short and Simple Prayers,
London: 1844.

GOODNIGHT
to the
JULY
BABY

SUMMER nights are mysterious, the sky is so full of stars and you perhaps have your window wide open. It is impossible to look into the night sky and not wonder about the new life you have brought into the world. What kind of world will your baby grow up into? What is it going to be like in the new century which your baby will most probably live to see? If you could have the traditional fairies at your baby's christening what gifts would you ask them to present? It's so difficult to guess what the best wish would be. Would you like the traditional health, wealth and happiness? Or would you like brilliance, or fame from personal magnetism? It is a sobering thought that if it were possible to wish, and that wish could come true, likely enough by the time the baby is old enough to express an opinion it will turn round and say, 'What on earth did you wish that for? I would so much rather have had –' And even without this thought, would you wish if you could, knowing it might change your baby? Wouldn't you rather say, 'No thank you, run away with your wishes. I wouldn't alter my baby. I'm going to love it just the way it is'?

Noel Streatfeild